In a garden full of colorful flowers, lived a little butterfly named Zephyrella . Her home was a paradise of scents and colors, but Zephyrella had a question in her heart: "Why do we have to be separated by borders? Why can't we fly freely and explore the world?"

With the first ray of dawn, Zephyrella decided to embark on a journey to find the answer. She spread her colorful wings and soared into the sky, leaving behind her familiar garden.

Zephyrella flew over rivers that twisted like ribbons of silver, crossed tall mountains that brushed the clouds, and bustling cities full of life. While admiring a meadow full of flowers, she saw a bee gracefully hovering, her body covered in golden pollen. The bee, named Aisha, moved with a precision known only to the most dedicated. Intrigued by her energy, Zephyrella decided to approach her.

"Hello, Aisha," Zephyrella greeted, admiring how the bee moved delicately between flowers. "I'm trying to understand why there are borders. Do you know why?"

Aisha paused and looked at Zephyrella. "Zephyrella, when I fly between flowers, I gather more than nectar. Each flower's unique scent and color make the meadow special. If they were all the same, we wouldn't appreciate their beauty. Borders try to separate us, but our true strength and beauty come from unity."

With a buzz of thanks, Zephyrella continued her journey, her heart beating with new ideas. As she soared higher, she saw a blue glimmer at the top of a tree. There, with his chest held high and eyes filled with the wisdom of many flights, a bird named Kaito watched the horizon, as if he could see beyond the visible. Intrigued by his penetrating gaze, Zephyrella perched next to him.

"Borders are like the branches of trees," Kaito explained, while looking nostalgically at the horizon. "Branches offer us shelter, a place to rest and observe the world. But they have always been mere starting points for me. Although they seem like limitations, I have always found a way to rise above them. Branches do not define my flight, and borders should not define yours, Zephyrella. Remember, the sky is as vast as your imagination allows you to see."

Zephyrella reflected on Kaito's words as she continued her journey, feeling lighter with each passing moment.

Finally, Zephyrella arrived at a serene lake where she encountered a wise old turtle named Akira. The elderly turtle was submerged up to her neck in the crystal-clear water.

"Hello, Akira," Zephyrella said respectfully. "Why does humanity have borders?" Akira opened her eyes slowly and replied, "I have seen many moons and suns in my time, little Zephyrella. I have watched borders rise and fade. Like the water, life flows, connecting everything it touches, ignoring the barriers that humans try to impose. I have learned that, in the end, what truly matters is how we connect with others, not how we separate ourselves."

With newfound understanding and a heart full of wisdom, Zephyrella took flight back to her garden. When she arrived, she gathered all the butterflies and shared her adventures and insights.

Inspired by Zephyrella's story, the butterflies in the garden decided to create a place without borders, a space where all creatures could fly freely and explore without limitations.

And so, the garden became a paradise of freedom and diversity. The creatures lived together in harmony, learning and growing with each encounter.

Made in the USA
Monee, IL
28 August 2024

64308230R00017